Whispers of the Heart Unfolded

Matipa Chivhange

DEAN THOMPSON
Publishing

Whispers of the Heart Unfolded

First published in the United Kingdom by Dean Thompson Publishing, 2024

Copyright © Matipa Chivhange, 2024

The right of Matipa Chivhange to be identified as the author of this work has been asserted in accordance with the Copyright, Designs and Patents Act, 1988.

No part of this publication may be reproduced, stored in a retrieval system, or transmitted, in any form or by any means (electronic, mechanical, photocopying, recording, or otherwise), without the prior written permission of the copyright owner, except for brief quotations in critical reviews or articles.

For permissions requests or further
information, please contact Matipa at
chivhangematipa293@gmail.com

Without limiting the rights under
the copyright reserved above, no part of this
publication may be reproduced, stored in, or
introduced into a retrieval system, or
transmitted in any form or by any means
(electronic, mechanical, photocopying,
recording, or otherwise) without prior
written permission.

A CIP catalogue record for this book is
available from the British Library.

ISBN: 9798326812018

Author's Note

This poetry book is an annotation of the perspectives I have. It explains the way I handle, view and deal with the world. As you read the book, I hope that it can and will inspire you to persevere and see your dreams come true.

As Benjamin Franklin said, "You can do everything you set your mind to."

Publisher's Note

We at Dean Thompson Publishing are thrilled to present this remarkable collection of poems by an extraordinarily talented young writer. At just 14 years old, Matipa has demonstrated a profound depth of insight and a remarkable ability to convey her emotions and observations through poetry in *Whispers of the Heart Unfolded*. This collection, her debut work, is a testament to the power of youthful creativity and the timeless nature of human experience.

Matipa's poems traverse a wide array of themes, from the intimate and personal to the broadly philosophical. Her ability to articulate the complexities of adolescence, the intricacies of human relationships and the beauty of the natural world is both moving and inspiring. Each poem is a window into her soul, offering readers a glimpse of her innermost thoughts and feelings. Her candid reflections on identity, fear, friendship and dreams resonate with a universal truth that speaks to readers of all ages.

The style of writing in *Whispers of the Heart Unfolded* is notably mature for someone so young. Matipa employs a free verse style that allows her to explore her ideas without the constraints of traditional poetic forms. This freedom lends a raw and authentic voice to her work, making each poem feel immediate and genuine. Her use of vivid imagery and poignant metaphors brings her experiences and observations to life, creating an emotional landscape that is both captivating and relatable.

We are honoured to publish this extraordinary collection and to support Matipa on her literary journey. Her unique voice and perspective are a valuable addition to the world of poetry, and we look forward to seeing how her talent will continue to evolve and inspire.

It is our hope that readers will find as much joy, reflection and connection in these poems as we have.

Welcome to the world of Matipa's poetry – a world of beauty, courage and boundless creativity.

EMBRACING THE CHAOS

Standing on top of a stage
In front of an audience
In front of a panel of judges
All with straight faces

I hold my paper
And the words begin to escape my mouth
Did I leave them happy?
Did I leave them appalled?

A girl like me
With the stereotypical body for modelling
With my low confidence, would I be able to
Walk without falling?

My mouth sewn shut
My legs feel numb
Focus, focus, focus
And that is how I snap out of it

RISE AND SHINE

"Be outspoken," my mum said.
"Be the head and not the tail.
Don't be shifted by the wind."
These are words that have shaped me
to become Matipa.

A little encouragement is all that it
took me
And boom, I have a book.
A question used to pop out a lot:
"Have you written a poem today?"

All it takes to see success is to
Put in the hard work.
Reclining on your sofa and saying
"I'll do it later"
Will not let you see victory.

These are all uncommon words of encouragement.
Don't seek validation; you just keep on working
Towards your set goals and don't withdraw because of fear.
Maybe you too could have a book; you won't regret it.

Just don't forget
That you are capable of anything
That you put your mind to.

FEARS

We, as humans, genuinely have fears.
These keep us alive.
It keeps humanity in check.
Without fears, there possibly would have been WW3.

We all fear different things,
But fear shouldn't set your limit
Nor sideline any goals you want to achieve.
Instead, it should take you to places you could only dream of.

I used to fear being left out,
Which is normal for a teenage girl.
But now I have learnt that forcing yourself to think certain people like you doesn't give you anything but pain

When you realise it.

And you start to regret why you even
chose to stick around.
This poem is to tell you
That you shouldn't force yourself
upon people.
Just be yourself.
Those who are chosen by God
Will soon make themselves known.

EMBRACING DIFFERENCES

In this world,
I think you have noticed
We all come in different genders,
sizes, and races.
These are our differences.

What does this mean?
It means that there are always going
to be inequalities.
One group, whether it be race, size, or
gender,
That wants to dominate.

Do we want this imbalanced power
for one group?
No, of course not, but that is how the
world is.
But no matter what the world's view
is,

Be the change you want to see in the world, just as ... said.

This difference should be used to our advantage.
Creativity and strategic thinking.
Let's embrace our differences as they make us
What we are today.

OPTIONS

Year 9, January the 9th.
This was the day the facts hit.
I've got to pick my subjects.
Where should I start?

Psychiatrist, psychologist, therapist.
Which one does my heart desire?
Would I have to go to university?
These have been the factors which I
have needed to consider.

Luckily for me, I had lots of support,
Be it from school, church leaders, or
relatives.
All were there to see to it that I made
the right choice,
And I am grateful for that.

Always consult and ask trusted people for advice.
Trust me, it releases all the pressure.
Choose because it will help with your career,
And not because your friends are doing it.
Focus, trust the process.
Ask, research, and think.
This is all I did,
And now I feel ready to tackle Year 10 subjects.

THE STREETS

It's dark outside.
By the way, I'm grounded.
The only thing keeping me sane
Is the art of poetry.

Street lights are on.
The sun has shone.
Now it's time for the moon to reveal
Its true beauty.

I look outside in hopes to see
The stars that glimmer and shine,
Lighting up the late, silent, dark sky.
The quiet, peaceful night.

The stillness of the night
Makes outside resemble a picture,
only

If there wasn't that darn
Black cat
Lurking by the bins scavenging for
food.
No matter how much you shoo it,
It always finds a way to wander back.

Each day I find myself wondering
how God
Came up with a plan to create such a
Masterpiece with his bare hands.

LOSING THE ONE I VALUED MOST

Oh boy,
Where should I start?
This poem really made me cry.

I think we all know who I'm talking about.
If you don't, then don't worry; you
Are soon to find out.

She was elegant, outspoken, courageous,
Generous, loving, caring, acknowledging,
Motherly, kind, respected, influential, loved,
The leader of the pack but most importantly,
My grandmother.

I always wonder to myself why God
Even created such a thing that would take
The lives of many, leaving families scarred.
I know for sure mine was.

Why was she taken?
Why didn't she survive like
Numerous other patients?
Why did it have to be her?

For the first months, it was hard to pray.
I think I had really lost my faith.
My question was, why did her great God do this?
But then the answer I concluded with was that
It took away her pain and suffering.

But in God, I found comfort, I found rest.
I found peace of mind and that made me rest my case.
All is done because of time, and it was time for
Her to meet her saviour.

My words cannot emphasise how torn I am
At the fact that an angel was stripped from the earth.
But to meet her righteous leader.
Rest in peace, Gogo, just know that the family still loves you.

CAUSE IN LIFE?

What is my purpose?
What am I here to do?
Am I right or wrong?
What do I, or am I meant to, stand for?

I am here to prosper in any given situation
And to spread the prosperity.
I am here to break the stereotypes.
I am here to rise, from nothing to something.
I am here to make my family proud, not only them but myself.

Are these goals I can reach?
My mind asks.
Conscience gives me a pat on the back

And reminds me to work hard for it.

My self-given cause is to leave a print,
Be different, and change lives.
And I'm going to achieve that through my gift of writing.
I want to be someone who solves problems,
Who ends people's sorrows,
Who helps people through tough times.
My cause in life is to shine and be seen for who I really am.

FRIENDS

These are people that you have found
Yourself getting along with.
These are people you talk
To whether it be every day or
occasionally.

For me, the word friend is not taken
lightly.
I have three main stages before you
become a friend.
Stage 1: an acquaintance. This is
where I know little
About you but we are joined by a
similar thing, e.g. class.

Stage 2 is being a classmate. This is
when
We just talk due to it being a
requirement

For me to speak to you.
Stage 3 is friends, when we talk not because I have to but because I want to, and I can rely on you for certain things.

I am gladly blessed with good friends around me
That I can trust and tell things, and that I can chat to
About general things and the relationship not
Being altered because of who I am.

BEST FRIENDS

These are people that I feel comfortable
Talking to about everything.
They listen, sometimes give advice,
But they are always there for you
when you need them most.

These are people you are not ashamed of.
These are people that tell you the truth
And not just what you want to hear
Because they fear your judgement.

For me, these people are usually
The highlight of my day.
They give me comfort, advice, fun times,
And entertainment.

I'm very grateful for my best friends.
We became close in the year of 2022,
And to this day, we talk almost every day.
I am lucky to have met such wonderful people.

JOANNE

If it's the first time hearing this name,
The poem is going to summarise it for you.
Joanne means God is gracious, and he really is.
She is the best friend I would wish upon anyone.

You probably know all my secrets.
We could go on a call till 1 am,
But you wouldn't mind or be bored of
Hearing my silly stories repeatedly.

You are a strong, loving, and amazing girl.
She sticks to what she condones is right.
She is not easily persuaded, but maybe put food there

And she might consider.

I have learnt not to make her angry
Because you don't want to be on her bad side.
She sees lions as big cute dogs,
And she is such a foodie.
I feel grateful to have such a wonderful best friend.

She has been my supporter, and my own personal entertainment.
She is a joy to know,
And she makes my day.

ASSUMPTIONS

Not all things that seem true or obvious
To you, are to others or in reality.
The Google definition of assumption is
A thing that is accepted as true or as certain to happen, without proof.

Assumptions, assumptions, assumptions.
I assume that people always know when I am
Being sarcastic or when I am not in the mood
To talk, but it seems not as you still get
Those irritating questions.

I assume that most people that are in

My life are trustworthy,
But as I said before, assumptions
Are not always true.

Friendships too can be just
assumptions.
Make sure that you are not just
assuming.
Don't judge people off of
Your assumptions.
Just like the metaphor,
Don't judge a book by its cover.

DIVING WITH DOLPHINS

The haters can sometimes be the people
That you thought were the closest of friends.
Keep your friends close, but your enemies closer.

They can be out in the daylight,
Spreading rumours
Of unwitnessed events, just to make you
Feel bad or be embarrassed.

Sometimes they do this and make us feel
Worried or unwilling to go to school.
Don't allow negativity to ruin your day
Or to put you off in any way.

They may try to tear you down
With words behind your back,
But just take it as if they didn't have the guts
To say it to your face.
Haters are just people that want to be you.

THE POOL

This is where I find my peace.
I can just sink to the bottom and the water
Will bring me back up.
The current of the water passes through my fingers.

My mind wanders off as I begin to imagine
Swimming in the ocean alongside dolphins,
Whales, and all kinds of marine life.
I begin to wonder what I will find in there.

The dive makes me feel like I am living
My childhood fantasies of being a mermaid.

The power I feel as I push off the wall.
The determination I have to finish the race.

I feel freedom of expression and I feel
It in the art of swimming any stroke.
Swimming just takes my mind off things.
When I swim, I feel free.

SHALL I BE A HOOPER?

As I launch the ball in the hoop,
I turn to my teammates feeling proud
As I feel as if my contribution
Has really made a difference for the team.

My biggest dream is to become a professional baller.
Imagining my name being associated with WNBA
Is all I do on a day to day.
Will I accomplish this?

In my mind, it is as if I can constantly hear
The squeaking of shoes as players run for the ball.
The amplified voices as players shout "HERE" for the ball.

The coaches on the sidelines
constantly screaming "MARK".

But this is all in my imagination.
I am daydreaming in class
About this ambition yet to be
accomplished.
Will I become a baller?

MY DREAM

I once had a dream
That I walked on water,
That I was riding a unicorn,
That I was queen of my own world.

My dreams are a way of my mind freeing
Itself from reality.
It's a way of putting me in power of the scenario.
I get to escape and reset the tables.

But then there come the weird things
Like dogs with no legs
Or the cats that hiss.
The mismatched animals or creatures,
I should say.

My dreams make me, me.
Or they are a simple translation
Of my conscious thoughts.
But all are my dreams.

MY RECALLS OF THE THINGS MY MOTHER HAS DONE

I remember when I was two,
My dearest mother threw me a massive
Surprise birthday party.
There was everything my little mind could wish for.

I remember my 5th or 6th birthday.
Was gifted by a trip to Spain.
I enjoyed it greatly, and we were always smiling ear to ear
As we wore our matching outfits in the blazing sun.

I remember since birth
I was always blessed by having food on the table,

Ready to eat, made steaming hot and fresh from the pot.
My mum can practically call herself a chef.

I know for a fact that my mum
Is strong, independent, loving, and many more.
But I appreciate the things that she has done for me,
And I hope to someday take care of her as she has for me.

MOTHER NATURE

The beauty of nature is unexplainable.
It captures your eyes without permission.
In a snap of a finger, you are gone,
Fully consumed by all its glory.

Nature gives me peace of mind,
Just the fresh breeze of oxygen to cleanse your lungs.
The fresh flower field to run through whilst you imagine
You're in a movie about escaping to paradise.

There are no fake or artificial objects in the frame.
From flowers to trees down to insects.
You feel free, or a sense of relief fills you.

A smile appears on your face.

Now it's time to go back home.
You wish that you could stay and
keep your mind off things.
But don't worry, no matter how many
times you go and see it,
You will always adore the beauty of
mother nature.

CAPTIVITY

Being held captive is so terrifying.
But I'm being held captive by my mind
As it fills with words to write, thoughts to think,
And dreams to turn into reality.

I'm zoned out into my own outer space.
I am the first to place the flag on my moon.
I bounce off asteroids of ideas.
I swim in rivers of knowledge.

Waterfalls of dreams cascade down mountains
Of memories landing in valleys
Of accomplishments.

I walk on each negative thought and look up
To the positive affirmations.

As I said, I am being held captive in my mind.
I can't escape, but sometimes I don't
Want to get lost in myself.

BEING RAISED BY ONE

Those who haven't experienced the feeling of coming home to one,
Living with one, being cared for by one,
Cannot say they understand when you say it's hard.

The feeling of having to seek advice from one parent makes your mind ponder on what it would be like to have both still present.
My mother has seen all the ups and downs of it
The negative impact of not having a full house

I can positively say, as a child from a single-parent background,

You become closer to the one you are with, as it is most likely that they are the more dominant in your life.
Don't take them for granted.

My experiences haven't all been pleasant
but they are what have made me the Matipa Chivhange known today.
They have shaped and moulded me and have given me the character I have today.

Everyone's situations are different, but one thing I can say is, don't wait for a phone call that you know in the back of your mind will never come.
As humans, we all are going to want to try to put in the effort where it lacks
But don't let it be a one-sided relationship between the two of you.

The End

Printed in Great Britain
by Amazon